If your life story were a book, what would you name it?

"I'd always believed that a life of quality, enjoyment, and wisdom were my human birthright and would be automatically bestowed upon me as time passed. I never suspected that I would have to learn how to live—that there were specific disciplines and ways of seeing the world I had to master before I could awaken to a simple, happy, uncomplicated life."

Dan Millman

UNEXAMINED LIFE

THE ROAD BACK TO YOU

How to change when change is hard

Lisa Duncan

CONTENTS

Chapter One

I AM THE QUESTION . . .
YOU ARE THE ANSWER . . .

In a world that appeared to have everything, trapped within a life lacking direction, lost in a place of deception, where everyone is out for themselves, I sought to expose my own darkness.

As my three-year-old daughter rode her two-seater tricycle up and down the sidewalk on a beautiful sunny day, I sat watching her from a step at the back of the project apartment complex we lived. Humbled, brokenhearted, and emotionally crushed, tears filled my eyes as desperation began to fill my heart. I lifted my eyes toward the heavens and asked, "Who are you? Please show me your face, I need to see you!" Staring intensely, waiting for the Lord to open up the heavens as a loving and kind father would do, I cried out, "I need you. I need your help!"

Discouraged and disappointed, I sat for hours calling out to Him—but He did not answer me. So, I cried out for Him to at least pull back the clouds and peek out at me. "Just a glimpse of you is all I need. Why do you hide from me when my life is in so much pain? Do you know how desperately I need you—or do you even care? I know that you see me, now, I need to know that you care. I know you're up there. Do you hear me? I don't want to go on this way. My little girl and I need a better life and a better way."

I did not take my eyes from the heavens as I did not want to miss Him because I truly believed He would show me His face. "You're up there; I'm down here—now what? Why won't you show me your face? Why, why, why won't you answer me?"

Dropping my eyes from the heavens, feeling all alone, I called my little girl to come inside. Heartbroken and still discouraged, we walked up three flights of stairs into the apartment called "C"—our space . . . our "space of lack." "I called on you, but you won't answer. You hide from me—what now am I to do?"

Chapter Two

THE JOURNEY OF WHAT YOU SEE

D ropping all that I had in my hand, I sat on the borrowed couch and picked up an old Bible. I opened it up to learn of Him, to gain some insight—only to have my hopelessness turn to anger as I shut the Bible to ask, "Why would you write something so difficult that no one could read or understand? Do you really want me to know you? Are you truly a loving and kind God?"

I have no food in my apartment to feed my little girl . . . I thought as I prayed for just a pack of meat to get us through the day. I called on those who love me, and they too were in need. "I believe there's a better way, and I sense there's a better life. But what does it matter when we are stuck in a community that appears to be hidden from your sight? How am I to know you when everyone around me is lost, broken, and have no insight? You put me in this world—but I'm at a point at which I do not long for this world. I long for something different—I long for insight."

As my frustration grew, my desperation began to turn into hopelessness. I recall thinking to myself, "I can't give up. I don't want to give up. You created me—how is it that you're insensitive to me? Don't I have a right to know you since you are the Creator of all things? Oh, how I long to know you—but you seem too complicated to understand. How do I reach beyond all that I have ever known?"

As I continued that aimless journey, full of misguided truths, my little girl asked me, "Mommy, what's wrong?" With a heavy heart, I began to ask her forgiveness. "Forgive me for the life I have created for us, for the way we are living and for leading you in the wrong direction." That day, as I looked into her eyes, I began to speak what my heart longed to give her, but my eyes could not even see, promising her that life was going to get better—something I just didn't know for sure.

All I knew for sure was what I saw. How, when I looked to my left . . . I saw nothing. When I looked to my right . . . I saw the same. When I took a good long look at those before me—I saw ignorance teaching me its ways. Then, I took a good long look behind me, as far as my eyes could see, and that's when I saw it—how from generation to generation, the trail was absolutely the same—no hope, no vision, no purposeful meaning to life.

I went on to explain to my little girl that, even though we don't have a church family, we would find a church to attend in the morning in an attempt to find insight into this life. I can still hear her reply. "Okay, mommy." As she gently wiped the tears from my face with a loving embrace that said . . . "I trust that you will!"

Chapter Three

SEARCHING FOR SIGNIFICANCE

With no transportation or even forty cents to ride the bus, the next morning, my little girl and I began walking in search of a better life. Looking into her eyes that day, I could hear her little spirit say, "This is my mommy, and she'll make everything okay!" I was at a loss. But it was the strength I needed to make it through another miserable day. The only thing I had was a hunger for a better life . . . and a thirst for a God who seemed so far away.

Now, in recounting my experience, I cannot help but revisit that powerful feeling that I had—a feeling that was so tangible, as if God was just one step in front of me. He felt so close, yet, He seemed so far away. It felt as though he was challenging me to intensify my pursuit of Him— a hunger and thirst for change kept me seeking a relationship with Him.

Arriving a bit early at a nearby church, I decided to sit and wait to see if anyone would show up. The way the church looked . . . from the abandoned houses around it, to the little storefront church step I sat upon—I wasn't sure.

I remember being so frustrated by the fact that I couldn't see or reach out to Him. Yet, somehow, He'd always allow me to know that He was there and that my search for Him was not in vain.

As time ticked by, a gentleman finally arrived. And without uttering a word, he unlocked the door and led us inside. I looked into his eyes, hoping to find a glimpse of hope—but no such luck—I saw no sign of real life.

Trapped in a community that lacked the will to respond—I sat gazing outside of an open window as my daughter sat quietly by my side. A bright and sunny day it was . . . the wind gently blowing as the sun warmed my face. Everything appeared nice and bright, but something was very wrong—something was going on inside of me. I could hear a gentle whisper saying,

"Life . . . is not meant to be lived this way. Something vital is missing."

Although my life lacked many things, I knew this precious whisper wasn't speaking of anything superficial. It was deeper than that!

Finally, about six others came, and the church service began. Crying uncontrollably for a better way, I remember wiping tears from my face through the whole service without any Kleenex.

After the leader dismissed service, a lady approached me to ask my name. Her next question was, "Do you like a big church or a small church?" Looking around and not wanting to offend anyone, I replied, "A small church." She stated she did as well. To this day, that question still lingers in my mind because that was the furthest thing from my heart. My problem wasn't in choosing a small church or a large church. My problem was I did not know the Builder of the church—large or small. To me, I just wanted to know the Jesus, who everyone had been talking about, no matter what size of building He came in.

I left church service that day more confused and frustrated than ever because I felt as if it was the one place holding the answers to life. Although part of my frustration stemmed from me not knowing or being able to communicate exactly what it was, I was searching for. I clearly knew enough to know what I was not looking for—more of the same.

From the lack of compassion for a lost soul to the very question asked that day—it was clear—they didn't have it either. Not even the sermon that day inspired hope within me—causing me to further question, "Will I ever make it and was this my destiny?" All I wanted was a better life for my little girl and me. Was it too much to ask for . . . or was I predestined to live my life this way? I wanted answers to life. I was in no spiritual condition to play religious games.

Lost when I went in, I left the same way. I walked away empty to never return again. Two lost sheep . . . still searching for their way . . . in a world that appeared to have everything, trapped within a life lacking direction, lost in a world of deception, still seeking to expose the darkness in which I lived. I literally felt hopelessness creeping in my heart that day, as my little girl, and I walked back to our "space of lack." Yes . . . that Section 8 apartment called "C."

"The human spirit is a metaphor to some and a reality for others. The human spirit is a combination of hope, will, perseverance, and strength. ... A human spirit can be put through trial after hurdle after trial and, although scathed, it will persevere. The human spirit is very resilient, it can be broken but not easily."

Chapter Four

CARRY ME

So, with my mind cloudy and the meaning of my life unclear, I continued to strive to enter in. Because something deep within me knew, that out of all the things I could ever hope for (amid the turmoil all around me), there was nothing that could compare to the peace and surety I'd longed for. And looking around at all the beauty, I could clearly see God there. Someone was smiling on those dandelions as they stood bright and beautiful by the roadside. Looking up to heaven, I began to wonder if my search for God was in vain. I hoped against hope that something would happen or even change.

In a moment of despair, I began pondering upon life: God . . . you give a fish water; you give a sunflower sun, but that which I need most—I am left deprived of. It was the worst feeling I ever felt—alive but having no meaning to life. I was reminded of the words of the late Dr. Myles Munroe who said, "The greatest tragedy in life is not death, but the greatest tragedy in life is living life without a purpose." Hmm—to live life and not know why!

"The heavens declare the glory of God; the skies proclaim the work of his hands. Day after day they pour forth speech; night after night

they reveal knowledge. They have no speech; they use no words; no sound is heard from them. Yet their voice goes out into all the earth, their words to the ends of the world. In the heavens God has pitched a tent for the sun" (Psalm 19:1–4)

If the wind can carry the butterfly, why won't God allow it to blow and carry me? I want to flow in my purpose! I want to smile and feel special, just like everything He touches! I just want God to notice me. But, where do I go from here when tomorrow is always knocking at my door—with the same problems, the same fears, and the same uncertainties? How do I rise above this? How do I find my way? I'm confused about my worth and blinded to my purpose—I just long to make sense of it all!

With not a care in the world, my little girl was blissfully unaware of the fact that each step we took represented the redundancy of the ticking clock of our lives. Our clock ticked no differently than that of the old blinded drunk laid out in the street—no hopes, no dreams, no meaning to this thing called life. The air we were taking in was no different than the air he was breathing.

My life was bankrupt! It was like going to the bank to withdraw five dollars from an already negative account—not a hope or a prayer for a better tomorrow. I had nothing to offer. I had nothing to give. I was to give direction to my little girl with no direction at all for myself. This broke my heart. I was blind, but yet, I was responsible for leading and shaping the heart and mind of this precious little life of mine . . . when it was clear that I needed the same. My little girl believed in me. She believed in someone who was just as lost, aimless, and uninformed about life and its meaning, as she was. It was a case of the blind leading and being held accountable for the blind. Who in the world would allow this to be, when it is clear, that the essence of life is growth? I sought a way out of this kind of life—a life that seemed separated from your kindness and hidden from your thoughts.

Deep within, I wanted to raise her differently from how I had been raised, because she too would one day grow up. I wanted so much more for her. Most of all, I wanted my life to represent a positive example of a greater and more promising life than the one I had been handed. But I was clueless on how to achieve this—how to grow, how to explore, how to conquer my fears, and, more importantly, how to become more of the woman I desired to be.

How do I inspire, with nothing to work with, not even a wise friend—how do I gain the know-how to rise above, when life is full of dysfunction . . . continually repeating itself—day after day after day? Can you show me what life really means . . . and tell me if mine truly matters?

> *"Come to me, all you who are weary and burdened, and I will give you rest. Take my yoke upon you and learn from me, for I am gentle and humble in heart, and you will find rest for your souls. For my yoke is easy, and my burden is light." Matthew 11:28-30*

You see, if your greatest influences in life are ignorant, how are you to rise above that and move beyond it to a more meaningful and successful way? Also, when you do finally realize that the way you've been shown has left you ill-prepared for life, where do you go when your comprehension about life is low? When the conversations around you are meaningless and no more than idle chitchat—lacking inspiration and a clear plan that'll help you win?

Staring off into that summer blue sky, I inquired of my life. Where do I go from here? Where do I go to see the light—when darkness and dysfunction rule the day? Where do you go for direction? Where do you go for guidance? Where do you go for instruction? Where do you go for a glimpse of hope?

Watching my little girl that day made me realize several things: just because a person lives a life of untruths—blind, ignorant, and deceived, lacking principles or any standards for their life—doesn't stop others from following them and adopting their ways as a reality of their own. No matter how sophisticated (or otherwise) bad traits may be presented, even when those ways are wicked, twisted, and perverted—one thing's for certain . . . One can always find an audience who will believe in them too. In my case, my audience was my little girl, and this grieved me, as it highlighted several questions in my mind. If I taught my little girl all I knew; I'd merely be teaching her the error of my ways, causing her to adopt my lifestyle and the philosophy guiding it, as her own. How can I show her the way, when I don't even know it myself?

> *"Like arrows in the hand of a warrior, so are the children of one's youth" Ps. 127:4*

What good is this life when the way you take leads to nowhere? And what good is it to be a part of someone's life, when in the end you are no better off than you were before? What good is love where truth is never known, and true love is never discovered? What good is it to have relationship after relationship, if, at the end of each journey, there was no game plan to moved you forward, no basic commitment to building anything meaningful and lasting together? Is life as a piece of paper tossing to and fro in the wind, finding no meaningful place when the wind settles?

Chapter Five

THE LIFE YOU LIVE

About this time, an elderly lady who lived on the ground floor in the Section 8 apartment called "D"—her space of lack—was moving out and into a senior citizen's apartment in the project, which was a promotion for her. I recall thinking to myself, "Is this all there is to life—to live your whole life in lack only to get promoted to more lack?" Although she was excited about her promotion and happy about what appeared to be her moment of glory, I wasn't looking forward to that. I was happy for her because she felt she was happy—but I didn't want to live my life that way, sitting around day after day waiting on a government assistance check that came once a month, and her first stop—a liquor store to cash her check, buy alcohol and a couple of packs of cigarettes.

I thought to myself, there has to be more to life than this! Surely, life has more to offer than to leave your family with a pile of debt, and some dry bones, when you expire. I believe it was Mark Twain who said, "History doesn't repeat itself, but it sure does rhyme." What a disappointment!

Where in this big old world, do you go for direction when everyone around you lacks the motivation to see and live life differently? I've heard of shackles on the feet and hands but shackled in the mind? I wanted a more promising future than the realities playing out in front of me. But what do you do when you don't know what to do? Do I look to her for inspiration and guidance, or do I sit idly by and observe from a distance, hoping and pray that my life doesn't rhyme with hers? How do you gain the courage to challenge such dysfunction? I couldn't help but allow her life to serve as a powerful motivator and example on how not to be.

I realized that sometimes you just have to take yourself out of the dysfunctional game of life to create a game plan that works for you. I had to become active in my own change in order to be better, do better, and have better. And in order to put myself in a position to become to others what no one was to me. An example.

Sometimes, you have to do all you can to challenge your own dysfunctional reality. Removing all excuses from the table and take action. It was as if my life and everything I had ever known was a lie. It was taking a toll on my mind and my soul. In searching for a better life, life, to me, became all about finding the truth. Not just any old truth as I had known truth to be, or someone else's truth as they knew it to be. I had no more room in my life for what I call darkness. Darkness is as ignorance, and light is as truth and knowledge. William Shakespeare said, "there is no darkness but ignorance." *"Like a lamp (knowledge), dispelling the darkness of ignorance."* Dalai Lama

"Knowledge removes the darkness of ignorance and thus helps even the most ignorant man to become knowledgeable."- Sam Veda

This actually brings to mind a woman I once worked with. She retired, struggling to make a $200 monthly car note, on a used 1990 Mitsubishi Galant! She worked at that company for over thirty years, and she retired without even owning a home or the title to the old beat-up car she got at a pay-here-buy-here lot. I saw her putt-putt out of the parking lot off into retirement, with nothing more than her used car and a few boxes in the back.

Everyone was cheering her on, but not me. I had questions, as reality again smacked me in my face. I was grieved. I couldn't believe it. I walked back into the office that day with a sense of dread. I remembered thinking to myself, how could it be that this sixty-something-year-old woman was a part of the latest statistics in the never-ending struggle of the common rat race? Getting to the end of her working journey and looking into her basket, only to find it empty. Sadly, the whole time I worked with her, she had been depressed, living a life of regret, unfulfilled and irritable about her life and relationships.

Whatever the case, I refused to buy into that plan. People are unable to enjoy life because they failed to properly prepare and plan for a more attractive life and financial portfolio. Paying the price for trusting in the common way.

It's a horrible and vicious cycle. Over thirty years later, I'm watching the same scenario play out today. However, today, I believe it's on a more depressing level. I'm seeing people work thirty and forty years on a job, and end up retiring with less than what they had when they first started. It is very frustrating and absolutely heartbreaking seeing people retire and not even own a home clear and free, nor have enough money in the bank to support them for the rest of their lives because they failed at preparing themselves while they had the strength, potential, and the grace to do so.

To think my life just might play out the same wasn't a good feeling. Conscious of my life, I could see the possibility behind Mark Twain's statement, "A favorite theory of mine—to wit, no occurrence is sole and solitary, but is merely a repetition of a thing which has happened before, and perhaps often."

People are getting to the end of their working journey, only to discover that the system they bought into, predestined them for failure—guaranteeing them a dirt-poor life—leading them to accumulate very little or nothing at all in the way of financial assets and stability.

I heard it said, study life and people. To me, that occurrence provided me with instant feedback. Life provides us with much wisdom . . . if we'd only pay attention. "No occurrence is sole and solitary, but is merely a repetition of a thing which has happened before, and perhaps often."

No way am I trying to focus on things—I totally get that life is more than stuff. I am attached to nothing here on earth that I can't live without. And don't get me wrong, I understand, if that's where you are in life and all things considered this is a step-up, again I get that too. I only wanted to know how I could break free from the grip of ignorance, poverty, and the lack of a game plan, which has consistently led to a defeated life. It motivated me to start thinking out the box and really hard about what I could

do, what I could become, and what I could achieve that would help me to live in a more successful reality. Because while I am here, I do want to level up my thinking and cultivate my dreams and foster my purpose in life.

Chapter Six

NO MORE GAMES, GIMMICKS, TRICKERY OR TACTICS

Several months after the old lady moved out, someone eventually moved into the ground-floor apartment called "D." One day, as I took my little girl out to play, I heard strange sounds coming from that apartment. I knew eavesdropping wasn't polite, but curious to know what was going on inside, I could not help myself. So, I quietly walked down and put my ear up to the door. It sounded as if someone was praying and making some other kind of strange noises—resembling mumbling. I had never heard anyone pray and cry out to God that way.

The day came when we finally met. She introduced herself as Freddie and told me she had been watching and praying for my little girl and me. I was excited! She had a powerful prayer life and confidence in this God that I longed to know.

She took my hand as I took my daughter's hand, and Freddie led us. She talked, prayed, and answered questions that had been on my heart. She explained things from the Word of God that I never knew. I learned that God loved me and that I needed to accept Jesus as my personal Savior and Lord to have a better life. I had heard of Jesus and longed to know more about Him.

By the time she finished with me that day, I left with something I never had before—I left with a genuine glimpse of hope. My expectations were high. I was looking forward to what was next. She knew God, and she knew Him well. Her life ministered to me in a powerful way.

She went on to explain to me how Satan was out of line and that he had to take his grip off my lives. Bold, she was, but I loved it. My God, I loved her. My spirit was teachable. God knew I was hungry for change and He used her to help me.

She invited me to her church. The greatest experience of my life was the altar call. I went to the altar to give my life to the Lord. My life was changed forever that day. I felt the Spirit of God all over me—right there loving on me . . . removing all the heavy burdens and sins.

With my eyes closed and hands lifted in total surrender, I couldn't see anything, but yet, it was the greatest place I had ever been. In His presence, the atmosphere was amazing! The air was different; the freedom was truly free, and it felt as if it was already prepared to embrace me. It was a place where my spirit was willing, and the flesh had absolutely no say-so! It was a place where the cares of the world seemed to fall away from the weight of their own insignificance.

For me, the Garden of Eden was in God's presence. It wasn't a physical location; it was an abiding place in His reality. In His presence, I felt a safe place: A shelter—a shield, a protection from hate, harm, danger or distress. A place I could trust . . . completely.

I remember being very sensitive and aware in that moment; I had never experienced being as aware of anything in my life, as the reality of the experience overtook me. I literally felt everything within my reach beyond the life I so desperately wanted to escape.

That moment wasn't about anything or anyone else. It wasn't about anything superficial or materialistic. That moment was about reality. No religious games, no gimmicks, no trickery or tactics or any of the games people play. Being embraced, it felt as if God had always loved me. It was amazing love—not at first sight, but in my first abiding experience in the presence of the Lord.

Due to this experience, I will never forget what true love is and where true love can be found: So freeing, so true, so much kindness, and unbelievable forgiveness.

Reaching out to what I believed to be my only hope, this was a pivotal moment in my life—my moment in time—my opportunity to change the course of my life, my future, and that of my little girl. I knew I was in good hands. It felt like two people who had been torn apart had finally reunited.

Everything had to take a backseat to this experience. I found the Lord, and I was not going to leave His presence until He blessed me. I felt like the deer that finally made it to the water brook. I was literally transformed in that experience.

You see, when you really want peace—not money or a quick fix, not fame, and surely not earthly things, but true PEACE—YOU WILL begin to seek God for a better life—YOU WILL respond to and embrace change. It is said that people don't resist change, they resist being changed. I wanted to be changed. I knew in my heart that to get to where I desired to be in life, I had to give up things that were holding me back. I even had to give up the wrong way of thinking. And in many situations, thereafter, I had to learn what right was. The Bible tells us that we should examine our own life. It was clear, not all my rights were right in the things that truly mattered to me and where I desired to be in life.

When you truly become conscious of God's amazing love for you, you will begin to grow and change. The more you grow, the more you give yourself the power to change and grow. Change is a mandatory part of the transformation you seek. We must embrace growth and change.

"Happiness doesn't come from big pieces of great success, but from small advantages hammered out day by day."

– Ben Franklin. I love this quote. We must be happy with what we got while in the pursuit of what we want. Don't despise small beginning—the beginning always seems small. Trust the process, and as you do, life and purpose will start become clear.

Chapter Seven

THE ROAD BACK TO YOU

Growing up and living in such dysfunction, dysfunction becomes a part of you. No role models, no mentors, or progressive examples. I had to learn how to live right. I had to learn how to breathe outside of the walls of my dysfunctional environment. Looking around, you have to be intentional to rise higher than your environment. The devil had a plot, but God had a plan.

Finding out that the Lord did, in fact, care for me changed my entire world. His presence has a way of doing that! It was as if all of life's answers were in Him. Although my needs were great, nothing seemed more important to me, at that moment, than the place I had found myself. Everything had to step aside, all the internal pain, all the confusion, all the regrets, and the rejection. All that mattered to me in that intimate moment was letting God know how much I needed change, and how much I wanted to be a part of His world.

Although many times, I have found myself trying to explain the experience, there are just no words that I could use to describe what had happened to me that day. All I know is, I had risen outside of my dysfunctional environment and I found myself in a new one.

All I wanted in life was to feel real and whole. I had longed for it, but I just didn't know how to enter into His reality—His presence. I was so at peace knowing that God saw me and that He loved and cared for me just as much as the dandelions standing brightly by the roadside. It was good to know that He didn't see me as this foreign object or distant thing He created, neglected, and rejected. I wanted to know that I was special and that my life counts.

There is a story behind every person and a reason why behind every victory. Here is my reason why:

I remember the pastor telling me that day, "If you died today, you would go to heaven." That beautiful miracle changed my life forever. Burdens lifted. Tears of hope, relief, and freedom washed over me that day like nothing had ever before. I accepted Jesus into my heart, and He became my Savior and my Lord. I could breathe—freely. I began to feel good about my future. And you know what? That still small loving voice was right, Life wasn't meant to be lived that way. I've heard it said, "no one ever is defeated until defeat has been accepted as a reality."

One of the saddest things to me about living in a what I call a vulnerable community is, sometimes, the meanness of life, people outside of it, and the systems they have in place, have a unique way of making you feel less than—lost, without hope, feeling as if God Himself doesn't even care. The rejection—the betterment or better-than attitudes was so damaging that it actually caused me to sometimes entertain the possibility that I just might be a part of a cursed people, simply because of the color of my skin.

Yes, the meanness of this world will tell you and even try to make you feel like you came from a monkey, a gorilla, or something worse. But the beauty of God's reality and the restoration of His love, is amazing at putting you back together intellectually so that you will know without a doubt that you are more important than what others think or how they view you.

It was clear—the Lord was orchestrating my steps. My search for God was not in vain. My soul was at rest because I finally found the peace I had been searching for. I found the inner hope I had been longing for.

God set me in that church family for many reasons, and although it was a large congregation, the Lord used them to teach me some valuable and vital lessons in this walk, lessons I desperately needed. Teaching me how to become a better version of myself. My new church family was in no way concerned about what I wore—they were concerned for my spiritual growth—exactly what I needed. I loved growing.

They made it clear that it was all about people with God—be it a large church or a small one. God doesn't love one person above another—not even the pastor. We are all valuable in God's sight. What separates us from anything is our ability to love one another. God is love. And His ways are to be the focus of our growth. Not the building we worship in—be it megachurch or be it small. I love the fact that the Lord made this clear to me upfront—it saved me from a lot of idle chit chat and disappointments that leads to nowhere fast.

> *Jesus said, "A new commandment I give to you, that you love one another; as I have loved you, that you also love one another. By this, all will know that you are My disciples, if you have love for one another" (John 13:34–35).*

The big church vs. small church issue never came up in my newfound church. From my perspective, some things are insignificant in terms of the greater purpose for the reason Jesus came, died, and rose again. So, for me—big church vs. small church—I squashed that debate long ago.

I allow those who choose to debate the insignificant issues to debate them alone. I have learned that sometimes, you just have to allow those who want to sweat the small stuff, to do so. I personally take no sides because I can see the need and the benefits of both.

I needed to know who I was and why God put me here on earth, and what was His plan for my life? I wanted to know what I could do to live and experience a better life. I wanted to know my true potential, my self-worth, and not settle for anything less than what I was created for. I wanted to know if my future was brighter than that of my past, and even my present state.

This is why we are to seek first the Kingdom of Heaven and His righteousness (His way of doing things); to learn of Him and grow in wisdom, knowledge, and understanding, so that we may not be misguided or thrown off track by man's religious opinions and traditions—which makes the Word of God of no effect. God wants us to have a sound mind.

Now, whenever people ask me the "big church vs. small church" question, I kindly and simply say, "As for me—it is a joy and a pleasure to be wherever God is—be it a big church or small one—the Spirit of the Lord remains faithful and unchangeable, and He loves us all equally. The Bible tells me that the Kingdom of Heaven is within us. So, wherever I go—I know God is there." Even though I had two different experiences, I realized I couldn't judge the small church based on that one small church experience. Likewise, my large church experience doesn't represent them all. Bottom line, follow your inner peace wherever you are.

Trusting God for a better life was very new to me. This brings to mind my very first sacrifice, though, at that time, I wasn't spiritually mature enough to understand it as such.

Chapter Eight

THE JOURNEY TO CHANGE

Shortly after my salvation experience, I was riding home after church service with Freddie. She explained, "now that you've made a decision to live a better life, you need to get "the devil" out of your apartment." Yes . . . that Section 8 apartment called "C." My space of lack!

"I do?" I responded.

"Yes," she firmly, yet kindly replied upon noting my confusion.

She was talking about the man I had been living with. Although her language in expressing it wasn't endearing, I wasn't at all upset or offended because I understood where she was coming from and the reason, I had to give him up. I loved this man. However, as much as I loved him and wanted to see him have the same experience so he too could be free, he simply wasn't ready! And I had to be ok with that.

There is a quote which says . . . "Unless you are prepared to give up something valuable you will never be able to truly change at all because you will be forever in the control of things you can't give up." -Andy Law

To help get my life in a posture to be blessed, Freddie further explained, "Now that you have accepted Christ into your heart, God has called for us to put an end to ignorance and sin." My interpretation, "Give up the things hindering you and step by step begin to rebuild, change, and invest in your future."

Freddie asked me if I needed her help to explain to him that it was over. Again, she was bold, and I loved it. Now, many would not like this type of bold correction, but as for me, I loved it. Her passion for living a fulfilling and rewarding life, as well as the time and energy she invested in me, was a beautiful illustration of God's love for me. Yes. Her honesty was hard, but the rewards of obedience were priceless. Side note. Today, looking over my life from where I was to where I am today, it was well worth it. Sometimes, you have to end a relationship to get the one you desire.

I longed for guidance in my life—someone who could accurately instruct me in the right ways. I had never had anyone to take an interest in my life that way. Nor explain to me the value of loving accurately and wanting someone better suited for my life, especially being a single mother. Again, the power of an unwavering aim:

"Like arrows in the hand of a warrior, so are the children of one's youth" Ps. 127:4.

God knew I needed spiritual guidance. Sad to say, in the community I grew up in, standards were not honorable, and morals weren't something lived out, respected, or valued.

You see, some people will never allow themselves to get to this point because many are too easily offended. Therefore, the issues of the heart are never properly dealt with. I thank God for sending someone in my life that was bold enough to say, "This is not how you live it—this is how you live it." The Bible tells us,

"Open rebuke is better than love carefully concealed. It also says, faithful are the wounds of a friend, but the kisses of an enemy are deceitful" (Proverbs 27:5–6).

This is a powerful truth; one I quickly grew to respect. I needed standards for my life and sugarcoating my unhealthy, risky lifestyle would not have gotten it done. To this day, I don't like anything sugarcoated. I knew God was trying to shape my future—it felt to me like an opportunity to start all over again—to pick up some new standards . . . standards that ultimately revolutionized my life. No, truth doesn't feel good all the time, but truth and understanding truth sure does heal, set us free and have the power to put us on a new path.

Correction caused me to begin to reconsider and change my ways. And not one time did I ever say to the process or to Freddie, "You are judging me!" Correction is only seen as judgment to those who still love their twisted ways.

I had to learn another way. Being a lifelong sinner with unchecked sin, I remember telling the Lord one day, "Lord, I don't know how to live right. I don't know how to love right. I need your help." I was a product of my environment and I knew I needed to change. And I wanted to change . . . but how do I change when change is hard? From that day forward, I began asking God for wisdom.

"If any of you lacks wisdom, let him ask of God, who gives to all liberally and without reproach, and it will be given to him" (James 1:5).

"Wisdom is the principal thing; therefore, get wisdom. And in all your getting, get understanding"
(Proverbs 4:7).

I knew the relationship I was in was not healthy for my little girl or me. Although he was good looking and a nice guy, I have to admit that his main love had become for drugs and alcohol, and not me.

Ending this relationship was going to be hard because as dysfunctional as it was, I loved him. Although I loved him in my own way, I wanted a better life and a better love for myself. And because at that time, I was just as dysfunctional and unhealthy as the relationships I was in. And because my desire for a healthier life and love was stronger than the dysfunctional love and life I was living. I didn't want anything or anyone to interfere with my newfound opportunity to grow and experience.

Freddie was very wise and patient in her dealings with me. I had to learn to appreciate correction for the results that correction brings. I had to embrace and understand that it's not about my dysfunctional truth . . . It was about the Lord's truth, which, many times, totally contradicted what I had been taught.

We all make mistakes and turn the wrong way in life, and many times, life is gracious enough to give us a pass when we do. It is said, it's how you respond to correction that shows the level of your character and determination. Here's the thing with God;

Even if a man fails, something that is necessary until weakness is overcome, nothing is wasted with God. God will even use the mistakes to keep your purpose going for his sake and yours. God wants your winning story of you overcoming. That means if you fail at something, God will take that and brings it into the program in order to keep you on track. Much like my story. Remember, no failure can stop Gods purpose for your life. The dream never dies with God. And the strength you gain from the experience will forms a new starting point for a better and powerful future. So, don't despise where you are today. If you want true, lasting success in any area, you must undergo the process. It is the first step to get what you want in life—a better version of yourself. It takes courage to recreate yourself. It takes a special kind of person to push your way through dysfunction.

Freddie was strong, but she was not abusive with her wisdom. It wasn't easy transitioning from one state of mind and lifestyle to a better one, because of my lack of understanding. But the one thing I always kept in mind that helped me tremendously in dealing with and understanding what the Bible calls correction was the fact that I didn't know God. I knew of Him, but I didn't really know Him. I had heard of Him, but I didn't have a relationship with Him. I was unskilled at what it took to live life successfully. I had to learn new ways of doing things because the results I desired, required them.

Chapter Nine

THE MIRROR EXPERIENCE

One of the many reasons why I love the Lord is because it is a powerful thing when the Almighty King sees more and believes in you more than you see and believe in yourself. It is also life-changing when you get to a place in your relationship with the Lord that he opens you up and allows you to see and believe what it is that He sees, and why he believes in you.

The Mirror experience . . .

Standing in front of a mirror, the Spirit of the Lord interrupted me

"Look into the mirror," the Spirit of the Lord said. "What do you see?"

"Nothing," I replied.

"Look closer," the still small loving voice replied. "Now tell me, what do you see?"

"I don't see anything, Lord—what do you mean? What are you trying to get me to see?"

"Take a closer look," He commanded.

Staring at myself in total curiosity, trying hard and desperately to see what it was the Spirit of the Lord saw in me, unable to locate what was apparent—what only the Lord could see. He continued to encourage me to look deeper than what my eyes could physically see. I knew this was going to be a defining moment in my life—personally engaging in a conversation with the Spirit of the Lord.

Through tear-filled eyes, I began to stare deeper into my reality in search of what was clear that the Lord had located in me. Look deeper, the Spirit encouraged. Then it happened. The Lord showed me—me. The Spirit of the Lord told me something that totally crushed me—something about me that I will never ever forget. Something that forever changed me. The Spirit of the Lord spoke to me and said— "You are wicked."

That truth cut me deep that all I could do was to cry. Exposing the very reality of who I had become. I didn't like the woman I had become. I didn't like the truth of what God saw in me—a truth that I had not seen just moments before. Or, maybe I did. But because of the dysfunction around me, which was the norm, I had no standard by which to measure my own life—the woman I had become.

This was when I discovered that within every woman, there are two potential women inside. The first is the woman the world and her community shapes her to be. This is the woman that is often nurtured and surfaces first. Often times overshadowing the possibilities of the (second woman) and who she could potentially become—a true and wise beauty inside. You have to build your dreams off of the light in Gods eyes for you.

Chapter Ten

A WORLD OF MIRRORS

Opening my eyes to see—me, the Lord replayed the story of my life. He told me that I was wicked though I saw myself as okay—it was hard seeing myself through the eyes of God. "You are wicked . . ." Wow! Those words crushed me. All I wanted from that moment on was a new heart, a new start, a new life, a second chance, and a new way of thinking and doing things. I did not want to be known by the Lord that way, or for the Lord to end my story without having an opportunity to change my course in life. I wanted to live differently. I wanted to like the person looking back at me in the mirror.

"Change is hard because people overestimate the value of what they have—and underestimate the value of what they may gain by giving that up," James Belasco states.

No matter where you go on the face of the earth, no matter the color of your skin, we've all been damaged in some way, shape, form, or fashion. Though some people will say, "I'm not damaged, nor am I dysfunctional!" The reality is, no matter the community you grew up in—everyone has a dysfunctional story to tell.

The Lord showed me—me in a totally different way than I saw myself.

You see, some things are just so shameful that it'll make you avoid looking deep into the mirror. So dark, that you'd rather not share. So ugly that it will make you avoid facing you. Many of these things are so dysfunctional that it's easier to look away and avoid them all together.

Looking into the mirror that day, I began to see just how dysfunctional my life really was. Sad to say, the lives of those around me were just as dysfunctional as mine.

I know many may feel that the saying "You are wicked" was hard, simply because people don't want to be judged that harshly—many people live years without anyone challenging their dysfunctional ways to such a degree, but for me, it was necessary and justified.

When I walked away from that mirror, I began to examine myself. I began adopting standards for my life that day because I was forced to face the reality of me. I began to see clearly what the Lord had located in me. I began to repent. I didn't run, hid, or ignore it. I acknowledged it. That day, I openly confessed and did not deny that my life was indeed jacked up.

I walked away from that mirror, feeling pretty bad. And in the secrecy of my own heart pondered upon my reality and said, "I am so jacked up." And at that very moment, something amazing happened. The Lord, again, interrupted me, but this time, He said, "No, you are not!" I was totally confused—had a real Scooby-Doo moment with a Shaggy look on my face, saying,

"Lord . . . you tell me I am wicked, and then a few seconds later, you turn around and say that I am not. After you show me, me, and I began acknowledging who I had become—confessing my faults and repenting of my unattractive ways openly before you, you then tell me, "No, you are not!" That this isn't the way you see me?

Believe it or not, and as strange as it may sound (the dynamics of this paradox, when two opposites are true), it was the beginning of a brand-new love and a beautiful relationship between God and me. Sounds twisted? I know . . . but it's not! This is how the Spirit of the Lord loves you and me. Yes, *"Faithful are the wounds of a friend…" Proverbs 27:6*

Through the mirror experience, the Lord allowed me to enter-in to see the reality of what He meant by, "You are wicked." "No, you are not!" The Lord explained, "Who you have become, I did not create you that way, nor was this my original intended purpose for your life. I see the wickedness in your lifestyle. It's naked and open before me, and I hate it. But until you see the reality of yourself and recognize your own negative issues—you will never turn away from them and you will never change or grow . . . and the saddest of all, I cannot move you forward with intention and purpose with a spirit like that."

The mirror experience was the beginning of a brand-new life and love for me. A sad but beautiful reality about me—beautiful in that, I got it and it caused a deep consciousness for change within me.

And I must admit, confessing my faults to the Lord that day was one of the easiest things I had ever done—it was one of the most liberating and loving experiences of my life. It was the very thing that caused me to fall deeply in love with God and His life-changing truths. The truth will set you free.

The bottom line to the mirror experience was this . . . God was letting me know that I could rebuild and shape my future starting that day. Again, I could hear the gentle whisperer say, "It's okay to be jacked up, but it's not okay to stay that way."

To fully appreciate and learn from the mirror experience, you must understand this one vital truth. The mirror experience has nothing to do with the outside world and its influences. At that moment, it has everything to do with what is going on inside of you, the unseen truths . . . the hidden motive . . . the unhealthy agenda. . . the true state of your character. The mirror symbolizes the power of self-reflection: self-knowledge, self-respect, knowledge of self. Being intentional regarding one's self. Self-awareness and self-realization. Knowing that God has a bigger dream and a better plan for your life.

Looking in the mirror, you will be forced to dig deep— deeper than you ever have, to find the truer more attractive version of yourself. Yes, it's that personal. Because what you become in the process is far more important than the dream.

One of my favorite scriptures and I have many, is found in the book of Corinthians. *"Everything is permissible for me to do; but not everything is beneficial. Everything is permissible, but not everything is constructive for my life" (1 Corinthians 6:12).*

"Before you can control conditions, you must first control yourself. Self-mastery is the hardest job you will ever tackle. If you do not conquer self, you will be conquered by self. You may see at one and the same time both your best friend and your greatest enemy by stepping in front of a mirror." Insert from Think and grow rich by Napoleon Hill

If we only lived in a world of more mirrors. It is said, when looking for faults; we must use the mirror and not a telescope.

The mirror experience is all about you! To get you to see you. Whatever you do, don't spend your time looking for the faults in others but fail to correct your own. Self-accountability, self-examination, self-awareness, self-discovery all happens when you are in the mirrors view.

Authentic love is when the Spirit of the Lord comes to you and says, "Let's erase all that and replace it with something new. Let me mold you and shape you into the beautiful woman I originally created you to be. I'll deal with you, and I promise, if you trust and obey me, I won't be too hard on you. I'll bring you out healthier, wealthier and wiser—I will give you a new life. It'll be uncomfortable at times, due to your lack of understanding of me . . . and, if you stay the course, I'll grow you in wisdom, kindness, and love. Only then will you be able to see that it wasn't too difficult and that the process was necessary to bring out the best in you.

Correction does much, but encouragement does more. This is why I choose to no longer murmur or complain, blame or make excuses. I believe the Lord deserves so much more than that from me. And as strange as it may sound, I'm truly thankful for the life, the good as well as the bad I had to endure. I credit the experiences of my past, preventable and otherwise, for my inner strength to persevere in what was one of my darkest times in life.

I am who I am today because of the unhealthy life I once lived. I am who I am simply because when I needed to know that the Lord cared for me, He allowed me to experience the warmth of His presence. It wasn't my desire to stay jacked up forever.

God is a God of order, and just as He placed the moon, the stars, and the sun in their set place, God has a set place for our lives. God created us for a purpose, and if we try to live outside that purpose, we will never be satisfied. Though the road may be challenging, the rewards afterwards are unmatched.

Through the mirror experience and all the molding and reshaping, I went through, I've discovered that some of the things that are most beautiful about God are sometimes the very things many people hate. As I analyze my experience in retrospect, I can see now their astounding results. Because, again, the essence of life is growth. And growth is continual.

God will grow you and it will not always be comfortable.

Chapter Eleven

ASK. SEEK. KNOCK.

The face of God I sat and waited to see . . . I saw Him. God allowed me to see His face through His loving-kindness and through His goodness and mercy.

You see, on that beautiful day in the midst of my pain, looking up to the heavens asking and searching for a better way, I did not realize at that moment how much of a beautiful day it really was. I did not fully understand what it was I was asking for. My heart was just heavy. And all I knew to do was to cry out to the God of heavens for help, even when I did not know Him or understand His ways. All I knew about God was what I had heard—He was a loving and kind God. I had also heard the opposite; He was mean and would strike you down as well.

Seeing the face of God in my natural state, and in the darkest times of my life, would not have been good for me. I didn't realize He was watching my little girl and me every step of the way. I did not realize that as my daughter and I walked up those three flights of stairs into our "space of lack"—that apartment called "C," that the God of heaven was mindful of me.

We were His lost sheep. This contradicts the religious saying that creates a narrative that says God hates sinners. But that's simply not true. God does not hate people, it's disobedience that God hates. He gives us the simplest task on earth, which is to love one another, and we can't get that right. God doesn't hate people, He's too big for that. God wants people to truly love one another and to care for the next person. He wants us to help nurture back to life those that have lost their way.

On the subject of hate, the Bible says, *there are six things the Lord hates, and seven that are detestable to him: haughty eyes, a lying tongue, hands that shed innocent blood, a heart that devises wicked schemes, feet that are quick to rush into evil, a false witness who pours out lies and a person who stirs up conflict in the community (Proverbs 6:16-19).*

One day, I asked the Lord to explain to me why it is "He" hates, a "haughty eye." For the life of me, I just couldn't figure this one out because it seemed as if there were other things He could hate more.

This is what God allowed me to see. God hates a 'haughty eye' because it is straight from the pit. It's an intentional attempt to make certain people feel less than and to get them to shrink back from becoming who God created them to be. This used to really work back in the day, with people of color for example, and in some cases, it is still working today.

It was and still is an attempt to try and keep people in their places (neighborhood, positions) — a place where they believe you should and shouldn't be. 'A haughty eye' was designed to keep folks from believing in themselves—back in the days, it made them feel like they didn't belong. This is why it is vital to know who you are and where you want to going in life.

You see, God heard my cry. He heard my petition. Yes, the world rejects, but God lovingly and kindly accepts. I thank God that my lack of understanding did not stop God from answering me. I thank God that my lack of money did not cause Him to ignore or frown upon me. And the neighborhood we lived in, not even it stopped Him from stopping by to see about us. Oh, how I love Him!

I finally saw the eyes of God. He led us to and through the pathways. God parted the sea for me and led us to the other side . . . and now that I am on the other side, I have learned to never underestimate the power of God.

> The Bible says, "Ask, and it will be given to you; seek, and you will find; knock, and it will be opened to you. For everyone who asks receives, and he who seeks finds, and to him who knocks it will be opened. Or what man is there among you who, if his son asks for bread, will give him a stone? Or if he asks for a fish, will he give him a serpent? If you then, being evil, know how to give good gifts to your children, how much more will your Father who is in heaven give good things to those who ask Him" (Matthew 7:7–11).

This scripture came alive for me. I kept asking, and God answered my prayers. I kept seeking, and I found Him. I kept knocking, and despite being at my lowest, God embraced me.

God is truly no respecter of persons. Nor is He a respecter of race. But God is and always will be a respecter of humility. The Word of God says that God will always respond to a broken spirit and contrite heart. Brokenness is the key. It is the characteristic, the distinguishing quality to receiving the greatest gift ever—life and life more abundantly.

It was in my broken state that God allowed me to see Him for who He is, more than a loving and kind father. He is the Great and Loving "I AM!" All that I need . . . all that I long for . . . all that I am . . . all that I hope to be!

Through it all, I have learned to thank God, even for the no's in my life.

This is because sometimes, that which I want, although it may seem good, is not always good for me. You see, I thank God for His compassion on my life, for not leaving me in that dysfunctional and destructive state of being.

I wanted God to show me His face. Though He didn't show me His face in the natural state, which I was looking to experience, He revealed Himself to me in the spiritual reality I needed. Through inner growth, you only see God when you make a commitment and yield to becoming better.

I thank God for answering me in the realm that truly mattered— spiritual—the most important one. I thank God for providing me with the "food of life" that was more than just a package of meat. It was food I had no knowledge of.

> *"When the righteous cry out, the Lord hears and delivers them out of all their troubles. The Lord is close to those who are of a broken heart and saves such as are crushed with sorrow for sin, and are humbly and thoroughly penitent" (Psalm 34:17–18).*

Chapter Twelve

YOUR LIFE IN FOCUS

Inner change doesn't come just because we hope that change will come. Inner change comes when we actively pursue it and seek to understand thyself. Change comes only when we make a conscious decision to change—within. Change comes when we surround ourselves with positive, inspirational, and wise people. Patient people who have what it takes; the ability to see and the wisdom to help pull out the best in us.

The Lord is not slow in keeping his promise, as some understand slowness. Instead, he is patient with you, not wanting anyone to perish, but everyone to come to repentance. (2 Peter 3:9).

God is so patient with us that He will allow us to experience life's challenges. Challenges give us the emotional drive to endurance. Successful people are often defined by what they have personally overcome in life. As you go through challenges, stay focused, and grow through it, you will surely come out stronger, wiser, and better— you will have the insight to help others overcome and go through their experience if you stay committed to your process. Remember, the bible says, that God makes everything beautiful in its own time.

God will allow us to fail, He will allow us to lose, but he will never leave us in the process alone without a plan to bounce back better than before. He will even allow us to not get what we want sometimes in order to draw us closer to real reality and peace.

Some of the beautiful attributes of God are not necessarily those that make us feel good all the time. Those unfavorable ones like open rebuke may cause us to reconsider our ways and rethink the paths we take. His truths are deep and beautiful, yet many misunderstand the very character of God. Therefore, so many lessons go unlearned by people like you and me, which keeps us from experiencing more wins than losses.

Most people freak out when I explain to them that it was the open rebuke that enabled me to see the deep love of God. The mirror experience was a profound moment and message to me. If you are praying for God to use you, bless you, change you, help you. . . don't sabotage your growth by rejecting open correction by wise people you admire.

Through the experiences, I've learned that sometimes it is just as important to unlearn some of the things we've been taught, as well as to learn new ways of thinking and doing things. The process is for our betterment, and if we fail to think up in the process, we will live a life full of regrets.

More importantly, don't reject the mirror experience. Self-reflection is a vital part of the process. Again, always remember that the person God is creating you to become through the process is far more important than the dream. Where you are trying to get to. People all over the world are winning at life because of their personal journey of failing first. And stories of overcoming challenges. This is the winning combination and ticket. Your story is the new money!

Robert Kiyosaki puts it like this, "The process is testing you as well as teaching you. If you pass the test and learn the lessons, you get to go on to your next process. If you fail a test and quit rather than retake the test, the process spits you out." I know it sounds cruel, but it is necessary for personal transformation.

Although change can be challenging, it is clear, it plays a vital role in our overall growth and maturity. You see, pain invokes change. So, don't despise the strong hand of God—understand it. Learn of God and learn to lean in to his guidance. His strong hand doesn't come to harm us, it comes to teach us how to win in better ways. His strong hand comes to help make our walk attractive and the meaning of our life clear. Through it all, remember it is the results that we are after. Only then will we begin to clearly see the beauty in His teachings.

Funny how life works, in order to experience better, we have to go through challenging experiences. Your desire to achieve and obtain better has to be stronger and greater than the obstacles that stand in your way. It is said, tough times don't last, tough people do, and you are the strongest person I know. We must push!

As I travel life's journey, I had to learn how to not allow challenges and obstacles to cause me to shrink back. When going through challenges, always set your heart to learn from those experiences. The enemy wants nothing more than to make you feel like you are failing and are being punished. But that's not the case; in reality, life is actually growing you up.

Jim Rohn said, "We must all suffer one of two pains, the pain of discipline or the pain of regret." Growth without pain is impossible. The pain of discipline is short-lived compared to the pain and the baggage of regret. The dysfunction will never tell you what it knows best—that if you learn and grow from your experiences . . . Life will move you from losing to some actual wins in life. In the beginning, you will have to train your brain (mind) to shut up all the negative self-talk. The Bible tells us to focus on good thought. A positive way to achieve this:

"Whatever is true, whatever is honorable, whatever is just, whatever is pure, whatever is lovely, whatever is commendable, if there is any excellence, if there is anything worthy of praise, think about these things" (Philippians 4:8).

This will bring you to a new level of consciousness. The ugliness of the heart must be dealt with, be it publicly or privately (preferably intimately between you and Lord). Love it or hate it, correction is needed, and it is a requirement for change. Therefore, let every heart examine itself and gain insight into its own ways.

So, if you have not been challenged to face the deep-rooted issues of the heart. I pray that you have a moment of truth, such as the mirror experience. I pray that you begin to see and face your truth in the mirror. I challenge you to take a good long look into the mirror and ask yourself, "What do you see?" It is said, "those who spend their time looking for the faults in others usually make no time to correct their own." I call this their blind spot. Don't be the person that only see the faults of others but is color blind to your own.

"For the Lord does not see as man sees; for man looks on the outward appearance, but the Lord looks at the heart" (1 Samuel 16:7).

It wasn't until the Lord confronted me and challenged my ways that a better life began to happen for me. I began to understand the danger of not being conscious of the way I was living my life. Is everything perfect in my life—no. I'm free today because of open rebuke. Most people don't like to be challenged. But to change, you must be challenged. If you are never challenged, or if you have a spirit of offense when correction is offered, you will never grow, change, or find the inner peace you seek.

"If we don't change, we don't grow. If we don't grow, we aren't really living." -Gail Sheehy

What defines a person is not what is found on the outside; it is who that person has become on the inside over time. Looking into the mirror superficially will never reflect or expose the reality of what's on the inside of a person. Again, when looking for faults; we must use the mirror and not a telescope.

Question . . . What are you looking for when you look into the mirror? The next time you look into the mirror, take a closer look, and then tell yourself what you see. If you don't see anything, ask the Lord to show you. We can all be healed and changed, no matter the degree of our darkness and dysfunction. The secrets of the heart will not be judged by man's standards. God knows the secrets of the heart. They are not hidden from him.

Open rebuke opened my eyes to see me. Correction is a beautiful expression of love. Correction is actually love at its best. Though it is often misunderstood, correction can lead to true healing. Correction is always beautiful.

So, don't be afraid to face the dysfunctional issues of the heart—be afraid not to. You've heard it said, "God does not want to judge your sin, He wants to forgive them." Allow God to search your heart and reveal it to you. And remember, it's okay to be jacked up, but it's not okay to stay that way. I had to believe that there was beauty on the other side of my dysfunction. The mirror experience is not something you want to avoid, but face.

God is changing the way His people see Him and the way we operate in live. The Spirit of the Lord is causing people to wise up, think up and level up their lives, as they are repositioning their minds to live fuller more intentional lives. God does not want His people to see Him as an angry God. He does not want people to have a jacked-up opinion of Him. God's desire is that we know Him well. People are starting to understand the bigger plan of God for their lives.

God placed Freddie in my life to introduce me to a new way—and for that, I am forever grateful. Beauty for ashes—what more could I ask for . . . the oil of joy for mourning, the garment of praise for the spirit of heaviness. Life in Christ is beautiful! Only a person with a genuine love for righteousness could boldly redirect another life.

I will always be thankful for the love Freddie showed in winning me, a lost soul, for Christ. Her patience, her passion, and her wisdom clearly expressed how much she loved God and cared for me. Twenty-five years later, just thinking about it still bring tears to my heart. There will always be a place in my heart that will forever be connected to Freddie. I salute Freddie today for allowing God to make an impact on me— priceless!

When I explain to people how it was through open rebuke that the demonstration of God's love became real to me and that it was by the pruning knife of heaven that I received the greatest lessons about life, their reactions never fail—they look at me as if they just saw a ghost.

You see, when you have lived a life where there was no spiritual wisdom or any type of spiritual accountability, almost anything is acceptable.

Actually, it has been my experience that when correction was given, it was based on the natural consequences. It was never explained or dealt with in terms of spiritual growth and truth; instead, it was dealt in a way that kept you in bondage. For instance, we were told not to steal because there was no money for bail.

This brings to mind some of my greatest influencers growing up. They were what I'll call, for the sake of this book, ticket changers. Back in the day, they would peel the price tag off of an inexpensive item in the store and would attach it to a more expensive item they wanted to purchase. They were excited about getting away with it. Naturally, once the children grew up and got hold of that good idea, we too became ticket changers. In some cases, we grew up to become a whole lot more—taking it to another level.

Again, no matter how twisted and crooked one's beliefs are—one thing's for sure—you can always find an audience who will believe in it too. When ignorance is the foundation of a generation, something is bound to go very wrong.

We were more afraid of the eyes of the law watching than the eyes of God. It was a way that seemed right to man. We called it survival . . . living on the religious clichés and not the reality of "God sees your deeds." Thank God today, I understand the power of correction. Our souls did not prosper no higher than our thinking because we were thriving in sin. Many are still living there today, and they wonder why life isn't as kind to them.

I would eventually come to know the truth about those biblical statements,

"The heart is deceitful above all things and desperately wicked; who can know it?" (Jeremiah 17:9) God goes on to say in Jeremiah 17:10, "I, the Lord, search the heart, I test the mind, even to give every man according to his ways, according to the fruit of his doing." According to the Apostle Paul in Romans 2:16, "God will judge the secrets of men by Jesus Christ."

"God knows the secrets of the heart" (Ps. 44:21).

Never will it be my intent to belittle the generations before me or to bring shame to my family name for something I clearly understand to be the reality of every sinner. Sinners sin, that's just what sinners do. Nothing more, nothing less; can't add or take away. In reality, that's who we were. In our ignorance, we may have been sincere in making excuses for our actions. Still, the fact remains, we were wrong, and correction was needed. In conclusion, I highlight these examples only to bring awareness to where there was error. It will always be my desire to help others move beyond dysfunction to a more peaceful and prosperous life.

The bibles say, "It's the little foxes that spoil the vine." Foxes are those little things in our lives that taint one's integrity and character. And because we are interrelated, it is important to me that each person gains insight into their own ways. Generations are perishing because this kind of behavior weakens the ability of others to see clearly.

"There is a way that seems right to a man, but its end is the way of death." (Proverbs 14:12). Correction is always needed.

Though I had to stand alone and learn another way—it didn't come easy or without setbacks. However, the change did come, because, deep within me, I wanted nothing more than to change my life.

Which brings me back to the guy I was living with. Communicating this to the gentleman I had been living with and had loved as I knew love— choosing God over him was not easy. Nonetheless, I explained to him that marriage would not be an option . . . nor would it be the road we would be taking together. He replied, "I will not give you up for another man, but for

God . . . I will." Now I do have to admit, as dysfunctional as the relationship was, I would not have given him up for another man either. But Jesus was not just another man, and I was not willing to compromise my relationship or a better life for anyone. To me, it felt like a rare opportunity. The Lord was knocking at the door of my heart, and I wanted to make sure He had free, uninterrupted access to come in and change my life's focus.

The council of this world encouraged me to stay in that relationship. "He's a good man," my family said. "You had better hold on to him," many of my friends would say. Unwise advice has no regard for the dysfunctional life we lived. This relationship would have held me back in so many areas. Blocking blessing, opportunities and experiences that the future held for me.

I thank God for laying before me the option to choose life and for giving me the wisdom to choose wisely. When God says move, we must move quickly. A few weeks later, my live-in man moved back to Omaha. Freddie told me to believe and trust God for a better life for myself—and I did!

God began to rewrite the story of my life. After blessing me first with His love, joy, and peace, He blessed me with my first good job . . . followed by a brand-new car a few weeks later. For me, this was a miracle considering where I came from. I tell you the truth, when you purpose in your heart and give up that which is holding you back, God Himself will bless you.

Question . . . What are you not willing to give up for your one true love? Remember, "Change is hard because people overestimate the value of what they have—and underestimate the value of what they may gain by giving that up." Your life does not get better by chance, it gets better by choice. All too often, people underestimate the value of what may be gained by refusing to give up the very thing holding them back.

Sometimes, you have to give up a relationship to gain the kind of love you desire.

Chapter Thirteen

RETHINKING LIFE

From conception to the moment you enter this world, there has been an enemy (a force) who has been patiently awaiting your arrival. Its goal is to shut down and destroy the most powerful and loving relationship ever—that between God, the Father, and the crown of His creation—you.

This enemy, which comes in many forms of destructive way, is so aggressive at trying to destroy the relationship between God and you because he knows just how powerful and influential it really is. In fact, his pleasure in life is to devalue man— reduce or underestimate the worth or importance of anyone that God deems valuable. His great commission is to "steal, kill, and destroy" man's destiny, beliefs and love forever. And because this enemy's commission is so wicked, twisted, and perverted, we must make our way through all the inner conflict, confusion, and dysfunction this enemy has placed in our lives over the years.

Now, when I speak of the enemy, I speak of it in terms of anything that stands in our way or holds us back and against us becoming whole, free, and who God originally created us to be. I speak of it in terms of any person, place, or thing that intentionally alter our path, designed to keep us down and from becoming the fully active, realized person that only you and I have the potential of becoming.

I'd like to now share my experience of being sexually abused as a young girl so that you can better understand my story and how the schemes of the enemy begin to attack our purpose, love, destiny, and faith from the very moment we are conceived.

My enemy, like so many others, actually lived under the same roof that was supposed to protect me. And it did! It protected me from the rain, the hot sun, the winter's bitter chill, and all possible dangers of the outside evil world. Sadly, it was under the very same roof that, when the doors were locked to protect me, they actually locked me into a terrible reality I can only refer to as a nightmare.

By night and by day, a young girl child vulnerable in all her ways—mind lacking the wisdom to talk her way out of harm's way—lay naked and exposed to the lewd and lascivious acts of the familiar wicked stranger who had total and undetected access to her. While she played, he plotted. While he planned, she was lost in the moments of play . . . completely unaware of the darkness lurking in the mind of this familiar stranger, who constantly stared her way. An innocent touch, she thought. A nice compliment regarding her small girly shape, she smiled . . . not understanding the hidden motives of the heart or the agenda behind the games the wicked played.

After the attack, she lay dazed and confused, after all, that had just been said and done to her in the moments of horror and terror, unable to fully comprehend or communicate what just took place or prepared mentally to handle such darkness and all the perversion it warranted. The only thing she knew for sure, from that moment on, was, life, as she knew it to be, would not be the same or as kind anymore. No relationship will ever mean what it meant just moments before. She's a different girl now, not the same within anymore—and if she doesn't open up and share what just happened—the plan of this enemy was to make this her daily reality.

In fact, for many years, this became my reality. And because of it, I would live many years questioning the love and protection of those relationships around me, hoping against hope as many lovers came and went, that one day I could break free from the inner bondages and struggles imposed upon me by the unwelcomed stranger who constantly looked my way. Not knowing that the odds of ever becoming totally free were stacked against me. Yes, there are many survivors, but very few ever become truly free.

Although my family didn't know of the abuse until I was fully grown and with a family of my own, I never got the healing I needed as a young girl or the wise counsel I needed as a young woman. I was able to trace the root of many of my inner issues all the way back to that abuse.

It was because of that abuse that I lost my smile, lost my joy, and lost all hope. I understand today that, as a result of that abuse, I became so emotionally locked up and confused inside that I lost my most precious and valuable gifts . . . my voice and the ability to express the love within me—a love I so desperately wanted to give.

As a sexually abused little girl, I had lost my voice—not literally—but expressively. The devil played all kinds of tricks on my mind. The enemy had me mentally tormented. He had me thinking and feeling as if people didn't even want to touch me. That tormenting spirit had me feeling worthless and dirty inside—the reality of who he was. It was so hard for me to reach out to people and embrace them. He had me feeling that others saw my innocent touches as perverted, just like his. I hated his touches. I felt unclean, and I was bound on the inside because of his perverted acts against me. I thought others felt about me and saw me the way he had made me feel about myself. I became withdrawn.

As you can see, from the early stages of my childhood well into my young adult life, the enemy had me clueless. I had no idea how valuable I really was to the Lord, even though there were people around who would occasionally and casually hand out flyers and say, "God loves you" and "Jesus cares," it was hard for me to personally internalize and understand that love. Though saying "God loves you" and "Jesus cares," is good, and the reality of its meaning ever strong and powerful. However, saying it in a society where the true meaning of love is one of the most misunderstood words of our times—yielded, "God loves you" and "Jesus cares," at that time, impersonal and just another cliché.

The enemy doesn't bother me anymore about that abuse because he knows it doesn't affect my life the way it once did. I dealt with that abuse. . . and today, I am free. I had to face the reality that it happened and understand that I was not the cause of his sickness. In facing it, I gained understanding about how it was a direct attempt to destroy my faith, my life, my love, and my purpose by keeping me bound mentally and emotionally for years. I came to understand how in the midst of some of my darkest moments in life, that God's spirit was very close to me. His abiding presence was so much more meaningful and rewarding than the norm of love I had ever experienced. I wanted to love that way. I wanted to experience the faithfulness and the consistency of such warmth and absolute embrace.

I love the Word of God; it is so absolute. One of the most beautiful things about God—and there are many—is that He gives us second chances, regardless of our past. With Him, you can surmount your challenges regardless of their scale. You can create habits that allow you to love accurately and live out the rest of your dreams. He gives us the power to rewrite our stories and to begin again. God gave me a way out, and I took it. He freed me from the mental and emotional shackles of abuse.

If you are experiencing pain and just can't seem to move beyond it, ask God to help you. Ask God to show you His face—He wants to reveal Himself to you in an intimate and meaningful way. The Bible tells us that God will fulfill every longing within you. . . you are special!

The best advice I can give to anyone is to take what the Lord has to offer. I didn't want to live in my past. Even as a young girl, although emotionally locked up and confused inside, I forgave my abuser—I forgave him, not for him. I forgave him for me because I didn't want to make what he did to me my reality forever. I forgave him to release him from my future.

I didn't want sexual abuse to be the source of my anger or the motivation behind my pain any longer. I didn't want my mind dwelling there. Getting to freedom was very important to me. I did the work because I knew it was possible, and I believed that there was a better way. I refused to allow the dark moments in my life to damage my future or the possibility to love again. I had to do the emotional work. I had to get to freedom—no matter what!

The bottom line to the enemy is this, he is wicked and holds to no standards. Although I was victimized, I am no longer a victim. I refuse to allow that moment in time to shape the rest of my life or mold my heart. I will not allow that act of perversion against me to keep me feeling down, discouraged, powerless, or self-conscious. I made up my mind years ago to never make excuses about the abuse I suffered from the familiar stranger the enemy used to abuse me.

I only share with others, in an attempt to help someone else gain understanding and make it through their own inner turmoil. Every time the enemy tried to put that heavy burden on me, I'd simply reinforce his defeat, declaring to him that I am, and I shall remain free from his hold on my mind. I became empowered and took control of my life. Today, I only look back for educational purposes as I use my experience to help and encourage others.

Chapter Fourteen

BECOMING

"*For the living know that they will die; but the dead know nothing, and they have no more reward, For the memory of them is forgotten. Also, their love, their hatred, and their envy have now perished; nevermore will they have a share in anything done under the sun*" *(Ecclesiastes 9:5–6, NKJV).*

I have heard it said that the worst thing about hell is the absence of God's presence. As I once walked aimlessly through life spiritually alone . . . I found this to be true even amongst the land of the living.

In a big old tricky world, with a cunning leader, it felt nearly impossible to be restored after being devalued by the devil and lost in this world for so long. With no guidance or instruction, it took me years to sort through all the inner damage and chaos that comes from living a life apart from God that way. And in my attempt at finding God in that spiritual condition, it was so frustrating and confusing—so discouraging for me that if I did not have a "do-or-die" will, determination, perseverance, and a refusal to be denied; or, if it wasn't for my deep longing for clarity that created desperation, a righteous boldness, which caused God to take notice of me and help me find my way, I would have given up, and that would have been the worst thing I could have done. I would have hated to die in that jacked up condition.

The horrible thing about ignorance is not ignorance itself, but unknown ignorance. Actually, unknown ignorance is something to cry about—especially when ignorance, doesn't know just how ignorant it is.

As I grew wiser, I began to see the depth of deception (ignorance). I began to see foolishness for what foolishness was. Even the foolishness I had once lived and walked in became foolishness to me. Truth opened my eyes to see how foolishness and ignorance were no laughing matter—be it your very own or those around you.

Marshall Goldsmith Mojo says, "After living with their dysfunctional behavior for so many years people become invested in defending their dysfunctions rather than changing them."

Ignorance is one of the enemy's finest ingredients, with deceit being the choice meal of each day. His unethical kingdom made life even on the brightest and sunniest days dark. As for me, it left me feeling like a total bastard in all things—lost without hope and feeling, as if God Himself didn't even care. And living on that road for so long, I cannot begin to express the seriousness of living apart from reality that way.

I speak from firsthand experience when I say, "In the enemy's camp, he produces ignorant and unlearned bastard children by the truckload." I had to do something with my life. I had to make some serious life changes—friend changes, mindset changes. Our lives depended on it. I could not allow those same deceptive, dysfunctional, and destructive way of living to continue shaping our future. I had to make a U-turn for the sake of my little girl's future and mine. It is said. "you are born into this world looking like your parents, but you die looking like your choices."

This is what I have personally discovered. The reason deception is called deception is that those who are deceived have no clue that they are. This is why the lack of understanding is so destructive. The word of God says, ". . . in all your getting, get understanding" because people destroyed for the lack of knowledge. The late great Dr. Myles Munroe made a statement that caused me to stop and think on it, he went on to say, "people would rather be ruined than change." Let me repeat that. He said, "people would rather be ruined than change."

When the dysfunction in your community looks as common as the white on rice—you too will begin to feel connected to it and as if it's just the way life goes. In fact, when everyone around you lives similar lives, facing the same discouraging struggles, you will begin to view it as normal and just day-to-day living, because the notion that anything is wrong is vague to those living in it. Again, it bears repeating. After living with their dysfunctional behavior for so many years people become invested in defending their dysfunctions rather than changing them."

If you continue to personalize dysfunction, you will never come out of it. If those around you (friends) and those closest to you (family) are living in such a destructive way, then you must first acknowledge it, then challenge it and then begin taking steps to change it. Let it stop with you. I did not want to travel down the same dysfunctional path forever. Time after time, like clockwork, I saw how it guaranteed a defeated life. "History doesn't repeat itself, but it sure does rhyme."

If you are emotionally attached to unhealthy people and feel something deep within you trying to inspire you and draw you in a more enlightened direction . . . don't ignore it. Because ignorance doesn't have to be one of the options. *"Forsake foolishness and live, and go in the way of understanding." (Proverbs 9:6).*

In order to inspire others to do the same, you must come out first.

Someone has to stand and take the first step toward changing their tomorrow. Someone has to yield to God's call and plan for their life in order to break the cycle of neglect so others can see a better way and seek a more promising and attractive future. An in order to do this, you must rise from the negative and begin to nurture the greatness in you and not forsake it.

I have to admit, it was hard trying to shake off those dysfunctional and destructive ways. Being emotionally attached and mentally invested in an unhealthy community, it was like trying to sift through a pile of deception without wearing the bifocals of truth. It was like trying to find truth in a sea of lies. It was like trying to reach heaven while standing right smack in the middle of hell. No glimpse of hope anywhere in sight.

One of my greatest challenges was trying to connect to my most honest and authentic self. Because again, living in that environment for so long (without any good examples) had a strong negative impact . . . you learn to talk the talk and walk the walk of that environment.

As a member of a dysfunctional community, I can attest to one of the greatest hindrances of change and becoming well is when you try and come out of that environment to better yourself. Oftentimes, family and friends will begin to see you as indifferent to the dysfunctional norm. This is where many of those who attempt to rise above fall back because they have to stand alone and be strong. Many can't handle the dysfunctional rejection for a season and end up going back to that lifestyle, because, in a sense, it is comfortable to those we love and who refuse to change and grow in their unnurtured state. Deviate from the norm of dysfunction, and you don't fit in anymore.

In order to successfully move from one reality to another, it is important to have a mentor or a role model who can shape your mind and teach you the hidden rules of success and change.

As for me, back then, in that mindset, it appeared as if there were no other options for a better life available to me. Again, as always, I was full of questions and curiosity about living a better life. My questions to life became—how do I find decency in such hostile and dysfunctional surroundings? How do I find meaningful and intellectual conversations in such a low-minded reality? Trying to connect with people who could elevate my thinking, and where the power of open exchange of ideas is valued—would pose a challenge for me since I would be the one unfamiliar in that kind of dialog.

There is a common saying, "It takes a village to raise a child." My question was, "what if that village was just as unknowledgeable as me—who then will lead the children to change?" With no one to glean from, what really hurt and frustrated me most about those shaping my future was their inability to see the possibilities in aiming higher in life.

It was hard standing alone, trying to find life in the face of death, and freedom on a plantation of slaves. For me, it was like searching for the land of the living in the sea of the dead. A place where no one seemed consciously aware of their own presence there—a place where ignorance never seemed satisfied.

Martin Luther King, Jr. once said, "Nothing in all the world is more dangerous than sincere ignorance and conscientious stupidity."

I needed direction. I needed the type of light that shined in the darkest of places. I needed a glimpse of another reality, one that could teach me how to breathe beyond the walls of my environment—a dysfunctional environment created to throw you off course.

It was so bad, I remember calling on God at one point (on the verge) of giving up and said, "I need you to reveal yourself to me, because if you don't . . . I'm going to die in this miserable condition and jacked-up state. I remember asking, "Is this my destiny? Is this my simple truth? Was I created to live this way, or am I searching for something that just doesn't exist for me? If so, please let me know so I can accept this aimless journey and adjust to this misguided and meaningless life."

I went on to say. . . "whatever my fate—if I never find my way, if I never understand your plan for my life—all I ask out of respect that you created me is to grant two requests. One, that you not let me die a slave. And secondly, whatever you do—please, please, please, do not let me die deceived! I'm tired of playing this dysfunctional game called Life. If there's any hope for me, or if you have a plan for my life beyond what I can see, please show me—I seek understanding—I seek a better life."

Chapter Fifteen

REINVENTION IS MANDATORY

"**N**o significant learning occurs without a significant relationship". – Dr. James Comer. I would have never gotten out of that incubator of lost hope if God had not sent Freddie my way to start the process of change. This is why dysfunction is so dangerous; it causes lack and missed opportunities in every area it touches.

When I speak of death, I am not speaking of it in terms of the natural part of being dead, buried 6 feet under. I speak of it in terms of what the Lord allowed me to see, life as I once lived it and knew it to be—the valley of lost hope. Change felt too hard for me, to the point that I wanted to just lay down in defeat and accept it as my reality. Without the knowledge to change the course of my life, I was tired of all the dysfunctional blows of life thrown my way. I was tired of trying to figure it out all by myself to no avail. It was the first time that giving up had become an option. When I speak of death, I speak of it in terms of darkness, the lack of light in the form of knowledge. The Bible says *my people are destroyed for the lack of knowledge. Hosea 4:6*

It doesn't say bamboozled, hoodwinked, led astray, run amuck. It says, they are DESTROYED for the lack of knowledge.

At the moment of contemplating giving up, I heard the spirit of the Lord say, "I did not give you a spirit of ignorance; now go and figure it out!" And I did and still to this day I have made learning and understanding a natural part of my intention.

The world is a beautiful place. Sometimes life will place stumbling blocks your path. But you have to remember the promise. The world is filled with distractions, and the enemy wants nothing more than to keep you and me as far away from God's purpose and promises as possible. He wants to keep us disconnected from discovering our higher self and God's original intended purpose, promise and dream for our lives. Remember, the dream, the promise and our purpose in life never dies.

Above all, we must understand and protect our relationship and sensitivity to Gods voice to be victorious against the plots and plans of all the negativity thrown our way daily. Again, the enemy is wicked and holds to no standards to what's good, right, and true for you.

The word of God explains that we lack nothing to be victorious on the earth. God has clothed each of us with power and determination from on high. We must learn how to walk in it daily. To walk it out, again, we need wisdom, because the systems of this world are aimed at keeping us ignorant of our self-worth and abilities.

"His divine power has given us everything we need for life and godliness through our knowledge of him who called us by his own glory and goodness" (2 Peter 1:3).

Whatever you do . . . don't neglect to grow. Don't allow anything or anyone to stop you from achieving your highest calling in life. Less Brown said, "Shoot for the moon. Even if you miss it, you will land among the stars."

Lastly, put yourself in a position to win. Take control of the narrative of your life's story.

And know this, as long as you are resilient . . . you will be ok. The most horrible thing to lose is your will to persevere. Keep asking, keep seeking, keep knocking, keep hope, keep praying, keep dreaming, keep growing, and whatever you do—don't allow anyone to take your eyes off of becoming a better version of yourself.

I've learned a lot about resiliency. I've learned that your attitude and your individual effort to stay the course is the key. I have also learned that conditions don't have to be perfect for you to start. If you wait for everything to be perfect before taking action on your dream, you'll never take the first step. Any time you hesitate or have a moment of indecision, remember this—before every victory, there is always a great preparation.

Change is mandatory—step by step and brick by brick. The first step is to just get started where you are. Take full responsibility for where you are in life at this moment. God said, "I will order your steps," not your leaps. And the first brick you lay is to preparing your mind—remove all excuses because with God there are no acceptable excuses that He can't bring you out of. You have been given the power and the tools to change the course of your life.

I have also learned that as we mature, we discover many secrets that really isn't a secret. It's a secret to some and hidden from many others that need it most simply because they aren't looking for it. The rewards are given to those who ask, seek, and keep knocking for whatever you feel you deserve. The secretes are given to those who deserve it and to the ones who refuse to give up until they see change.

The secret that really isn't a secret is this; if you feed your brain ignorance, ignorant things is all you will receive in return. What you feed on, you put out…and what you put out will grow and come back to you in unwanted ways. Likewise, if you feed your brain knowledge and wisdom, rewards and fulfillment are what you'll receive in return. Because again, what you feed on, you put out . . . and what you put out will grow and come back to you in rewarding ways.

So, how to change when change is hard?

- Your desire to change has to be greater than your desire to remain the same. Most people don't try simply because the fear of losing is greater than the excitement of winning. Do the work and overcome your fears. It is said, "Do the thing you fear, and the death of it is certain."

How to change when change is hard?

- Your desire to experience something different has to be stronger than the strongholds of dysfunction elements keeping you held back and stuck—Be intentional at separating yourself from negativity, dysfunctional relationships and dysfunctional self-talk. You must be very sensitive and keep negativity at bay. Which leads to the next one.

How to change when change is hard?

- If you are not willing to change, then don't expect your life to. Stay well connected to things you are passionate about.

How to change when change is hard?

- You have to master saying, "No" to every dysfunctional pull trying to pull you away from your goal. Steve Jobs said, "It's only by saying "No" that you can concentrate on the things that are really important." Don't even allow yourself to stand in your way.

Like Yolanda Adams sings so elegantly, "Remember, every victory comes in time. You have to work today to change tomorrow. Remember, every step you take gets you closer to your destination. Make sure to reach back, use your experiences to sever others.

How to change when change is hard? This here is one of my favorites.

- You have to make peace with your past. You are your longest relationship. Start telling yourself what you are proud of about yourself. Life is short and you own it to yourself to feel positive about your life.

How to change when change is hard?

- You have to gain momentum, even in the middle of your struggles, whatever they may be. Learn to let your struggles fuel you. Commit to the process of change and never ever give up on you. Your greatest self will be made during your greatest challenges. The storms of life are not designed to last forever.

How to change when change is hard?

- Make it your personal mission to stay in a posture of growth. This world really doesn't have much to offer you in the way of true peace. You have everything you need trapped on the inside of you to make your life rich and rewarding. God made sure of that . . . Dig deep and stay connected to who you want to become. Everyone has a better vision of themselves. Whatever you do never give up on you!

Finally, until you find a good mentor, read lots of good books. Books have the power to strengthen your mind. They will give you a glimpse of what to expect on the journey. And, they will keep you inspired as you move forward. Remember, success leaves clues, and if you sow the same seeds, you'll reap the same rewards in your own unique journey. There are clues in books.

Within each of us, God has given us the power to mold and shape our environment— it is up to us to activate our own inspiration to change. Change doesn't just happen; we must make change happen.

Loving God with all of our hearts, mind, and souls is our greatest strength for standing. Discovering who we are and loving who we are becoming has the potential to keep you motivated and inspired to become better each day.

The cares of this world are designed to agitate our lives and paralyze our beliefs. Obstacles come to test us, and if we fail at learning from our experiences, the challenges of life will keep us confused and living in a constant state of frustration about our past and uncertainty of the future. Again, we can change our lives with the right knowledge and the right people in it.